**VAN BUREN PUBLIC LIBRARY**

8/96  Stone, Lynn M.  J/636.1
Blue...

8/96  Stone, Lynn M.  J/636.1
Back Roads
Blue Grass Country

| 1037 | AUG 26 1996 | |
| --- | --- | --- |
| 1203 | | |
| 1166 | OCT 10 1996 | |
| Kith | Dec 96 | |
| 1210 | FEB 24 1997 | |
| 1286 | MAR 17 1997 | |

## VAN BUREN PUBLIC LIBRARY
### VAN BUREN, IND.
**RULES**

1. Books may be kept for two weeks and may be renewed once for the same period, except 7 day books and magazines.

117241  Back Roads- Blue Grass Country

VAN BUREN PUBLIC LIBRARY

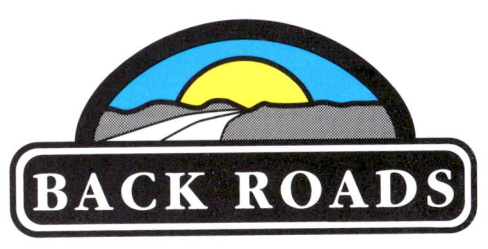

# BLUEGRASS COUNTRY

## By Lynn M. Stone

The Rourke Corporation, Inc.
Vero Beach, FL 32964

© 1993 The Rourke Corporation, Inc.

All rights reserved. No part of this book may be reproduced or utilized in any form or by any means, electronic or mechanical including photocopying, recording or by any information storage and retrieval system without permission in writing from the publisher.

Edited by Sandra A. Robinson

## Photo Credits

All photos © Lynn Stone except cover, courtesy Kentucky Horse Park; page 7 map, courtesy of The Greater Lexington Convention and Visitors Bureau, Lexington, KY; and pages 20 and 36 courtesy Keeneland Association

## Acknowledgements

The author sincerely thanks the following people and organizations in the Bluegrass Country for their kind and enthusiastic assistance in this project: Calumet Farm; Keeneland Association, Inc.; Kentucky Horse Park; Three Chimneys Farm; Vinery Farm; Dr. Jim Becht; Neal Howard; Nore Ghibaudy; Wes Lanter; Dan Rosenberg and Buck Stoopes

## Dedication

For Julie, Kim and Katy, who love horses

**Library of Congress Cataloging-in-Publication Data**
   Stone, Lynn M.
   Bluegrass country / by Lynn M. Stone
     p. cm. — (Back roads)
   Includes index.
   Summary: Describes Kentucky's Bluegrass Country and the role it plays in the breeding of thoroughbred race horses.
   ISBN 0-86593-306-5
   1. Bluegrass Region (Ky.)—Juvenile literature. 2. Horse farms—Kentucky—Bluegrass Region—Juvenile literature. 3. Horse-racing—Kentucky—Bluegrass Region—Juvenile literature. 4. Race horses—Kentucky—Bluegrass Region—Juvenile literature. [1. Bluegrass Region (Ky.) 2. Horse farms. 3. Horse racing. 4. Race horses.]
I. Title. II. Title: Bluegrass country. III. Series: Stone, Lynn M. Back roads.
F457.B6S76 1993
636.1'32'097694—dc20
                                                          93-23002
                                                                 CIP
                                                                   AC

Printed in the USA

# TABLE OF CONTENTS

1. Bluegrass Country ........................ 4
2. The Old Bluegrass Country ........ 10
3. Bluegrass Thoroughbred Farms ............................................. 15
4. Born to Run ................................. 24
5. Thoroughbreds ........................... 31
6. Off to the Races .......................... 35
7. The Kentucky Horse Park ......... 39
8. The Track in the Bluegrass: Keeneland .................................... 42
   Glossary ....................................... 45
   Index ............................................ 47

## Chapter 1

# BLUEGRASS COUNTRY

Kentucky's Bluegrass Country is America's kingdom of thoroughbred racehorses. The Bluegrass region of north central Kentucky is known for its tobacco, bourbon whiskey, architecture and sparkling bluegrass music – but thoroughbred racehorses are its signature.

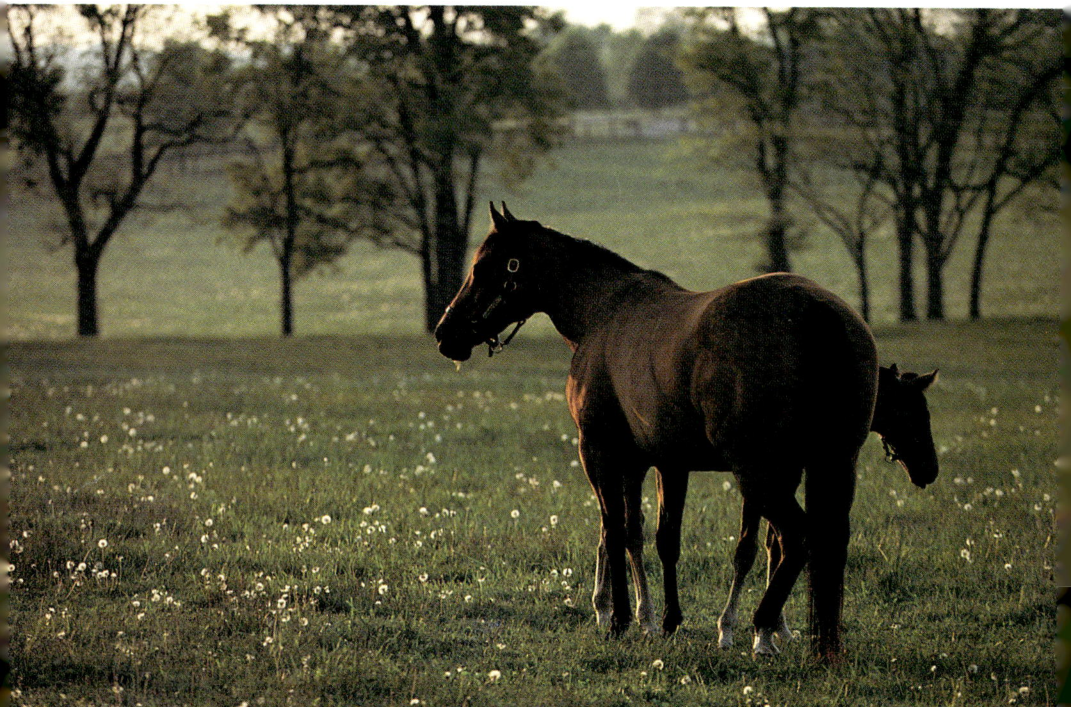

*Thoroughbred horses in a bluegrass meadow, the signature of Kentucky's Bluegrass Country*

In a melodic, bluegrass twang, a Kentucky horseman will tell a visitor that the region is the finest producer of thoroughbred horses in the world. The secret, he reveals, is the limestone in the ground. The limestone nourishes the grass and enriches the water with minerals. A horse growing up on such fixin's is bound to have the racer's edge, the man concludes.

The man may be right. The Bluegrass Country has raised most of the great thoroughbreds in American racing history. The ones it doesn't raise move to Kentucky sooner or later. Take the case of Secretariat, arguably the greatest of the thoroughbreds, and Horse of the Year in 1972 and 1973. Secretariat was conceived in Kentucky, but raised in Virginia. Kentuckians were quick to point out that Secretariat's father, Bold Ruler, was a Kentucky horse. They also noted that after Secretariat's brilliant racing career ended in 1973, he was retired to the Claiborne Farm in Paris, Kentucky. Naturally, say the Bluegrass folks.

No question about it: Bluegrass Country is horse heaven. But it's a whole lot more green than blue. The grasses do have dusty blue blossoms, and on late evenings and early mornings during a short period in May, the pastures glint steel blue. But on the whole, Bluegrass Country is mighty green. It is hard to imagine that pastures could be greener – or more nutritious. No wonder that some 400 horse farms are clustered within 25 miles of Lexington, the heart of the Inner Bluegrass region. Most of these farms raise thoroughbreds. Others have standardbreds, American saddlebred horses, Arabians, Morgans and quarter horses. With the numbers to back its boast, Lexington lays claim to being the horse capital of the world.

*Flowering dogwoods frame a barn at Calumet Farm, one of the best-known Bluegrass Country thoroughbred farms in the world*

# LEXINGTON, KENTUCKY AND THE HEART OF THE INNER BLUEGRASS COUNTRY

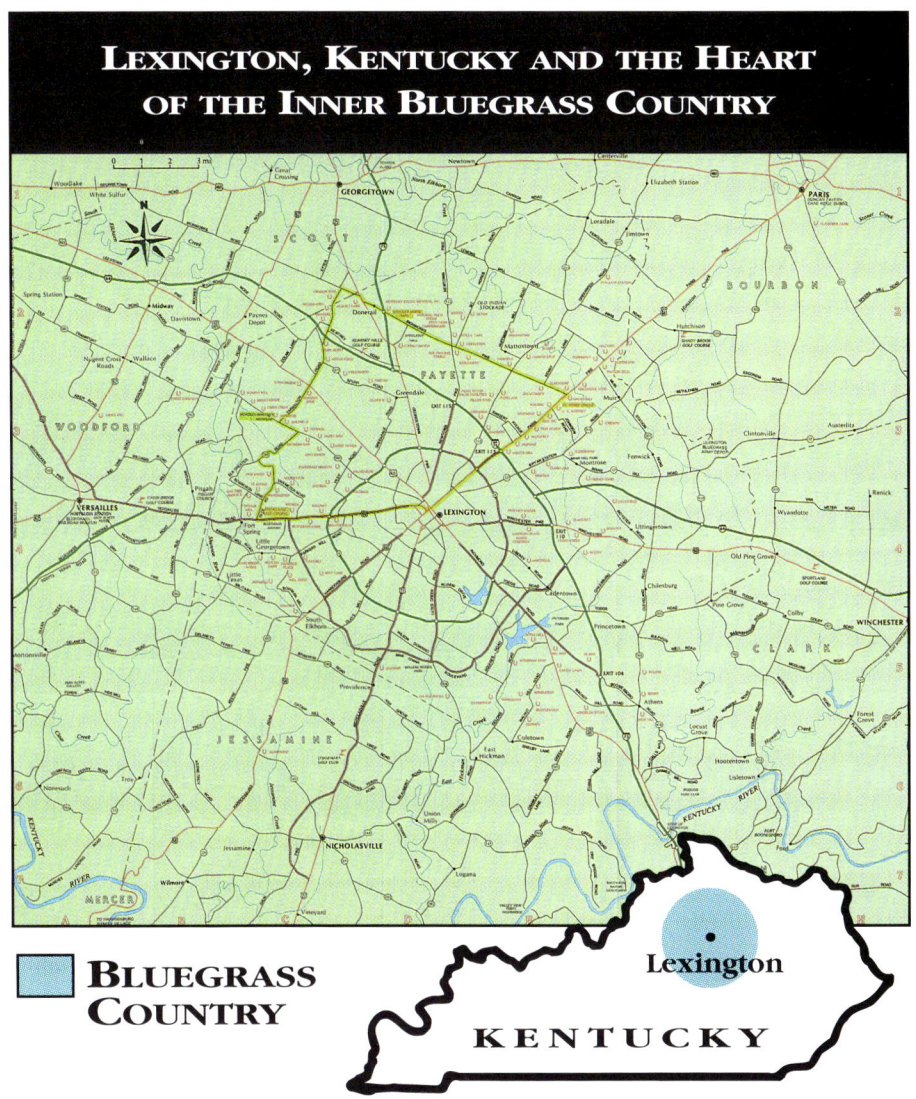

BLUEGRASS COUNTRY

Unlike the **purebred** horses around it, Lexington is something of a **crossbreed,** a mix of old and new. It's essentially a modern city with more than 50 major industries producing everything from laser printers and air brakes to peanut butter. Lexington retains a well-kept historic district, however, and still serves as a marketplace for the traditional agricultural products of the region – bluegrass seed, sheep, beef cattle and air-cured burley tobacco. Beyond Lexington, roughly 25 miles in each direction, lie the hills of the Inner Bluegrass region.

The pastures of bluegrass roll up and down gently, like scattered pillows. In the early light of a spring morning, they are the ideal landscape for grazing horses. In a more perfect world all the fabled horses of time – Black Beauty, Trigger, Pegasus, maybe even Mr. Ed – would have had at least one meal of Kentucky bluegrass and chased it with the mineral water of a bluegrass spring.

Towering sugar maples, blue ashes, locusts, sycamores and other shade trees, some of them more than 200 years old, flank the long lanes that wind to farm estates. Big trees rise from pastures, too, where horses laze in leafy shadows.

*Rolling bluegrass meadows around Lexington are a picture-perfect landscape for Kentucky horses*

*Traditional white plank fences have become a rarity in Bluegrass Country*

Some of the wooden plank fences around these pastures are still painted traditional white. In a concession to the high cost of upkeep, most horse farms paint their fences with a black, tarlike substance. No matter. Fences are fences if you're a horse, or if you're a robin or meadowlark looking for a perch. And traditionalists still find happiness in the craftsmanship of old barns and stables.

Here and there, horse farms give way to cattle farms, and fields of corn and tobacco. Villages spring up along the back roads, and wood margins hug the banks of creeks. Still, most of the countryside along these old roads beyond Lexington is an uninterrupted park of tall trees peppered with farm buildings, and thoroughbreds feeding on carpets of grass. *Blue*grass, of course.

## Chapter 2

# THE OLD BLUEGRASS COUNTRY

The modern Bluegrass Country is the product of more than 200 years of Kentucky history. Hundreds of the places that shaped the Bluegrass region are protected in 50 historic districts. The National Register of Historic Places lists nearly 12,000 historic sites in Bluegrass Country.

While Virginia and the seaboard states developed rapidly in the late 1600s and the early 1700s, Kentucky remained an uncharted frontier wilderness. Hunters and adventurers stumbled around in the Kentucky woods, but the first permanent white settlement, Harrodsburg, wasn't established until 1774 - just 18 years before statehood.

Just how much of the region was green with bluegrass in 1774 is a matter of local debate. The pioneers did not specialize in plant identification. There were breaks in the dense Kentucky forest, though. Some of the forest openings were **savannahs** - grassy, parklike areas with scattered trees. Other gaps in the woodlands were natural **canebrakes,** thickets of wild cane stalks. The pioneers certainly did not find the land in readymade pasture, but the natural breaks in the forest and the fertile soil inspired the settlers to clear the land for farming.

Among the **native,** or original, grasses they found in the meadows and woodland savannahs were bluegrasses. Many kinds of bluegrasses grow in North America. The pioneers may have found three or four native bluegrasses in the Bluegrass region. Later, through accident, design or both, at least four more bluegrass varieties were imported and became part of the pasture vegetation. Today eight species of bluegrass grow in Bluegrass Country. The so-called Kentucky bluegrass – known to scientists as *Poa pratensis* – is the dominant grass. Was it one of the native bluegrasses, or was it imported from England? No one knows for sure.

Settlers flocked to Kentucky. Many of them brought fine horses with them from Maryland and Virginia. Virginia, in particular, already had a tradition of raising quality horses. Virginians began racing horses in the 1700s, and by the 1780s, racing had spread to the new settlement (1775) of Lexington, Kentucky.

Agriculture boomed in Bluegrass Country. In the early 1800s the region produced cattle, corn and hemp, a plant used in the manufacture of rope and riggings for sailing ships. After the American Civil War (1861-1865), Bluegrass agriculture shifted from hemp to tobacco. The Civil War soldier camps had stirred the demand for tobacco. At the same time, the era of the sailing ships and the need for hemp were fading with the arrival of steam power.

The Civil War had a hand in Kentucky's growing thoroughbred population. Most of the battles between the North and South bypassed Kentucky. Virginia and Maryland were not as fortunate. The war effort took their best horses. The destruction caused by the war reduced

*Many fine racing horses were brought to the bluegrass by settlers from Maryland and Virginia who flocked to old Kentucky in the late 1700s*

their ability to re-establish horse farms. Kentucky's Bluegrass Country, still relatively prosperous, continued to raise its thoroughbreds.

Farming played a major role in the Bluegrass region's past. It may not be as important in the future. Lexington and other Bluegrass towns, as they expand, will nibble at

the green hills and uproot the old trees that give this region much of its character. The challenge for Bluegrass residents will be to find ways they can satisfy the need for economic growth and, at the same time, preserve their rural countryside.

*Kentucky's Bluegrass region continued to raise thoroughbreds after the Civil War had destroyed farms elsewhere in the Southeast*

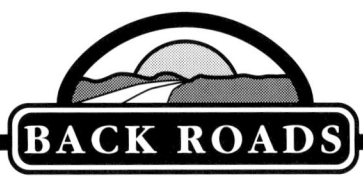

CHAPTER 3

# BLUEGRASS THOROUGHBRED FARMS

Life on the farm may sometimes be a long stroll in the sunshine and clover for thoroughbreds. For the people on these farms, however, the work is unending. Farm owners and their employees love horses, but a farm is a business. It has bills to pay, and it is managed to turn a profit. The thoroughbreds are the farm's lifeblood. Considerable human labor is invested to make sure that the horses are clean, healthy and managed well.

An on-site general manager, hired by the farm owner, oversees the day-to-day operations of a farm. On a large farm, the general manager employs several division managers, each of whom, along with his or her foremen and **grooms,** is responsible for one of the farm's divisions: mares, stallions, yearlings, maintenance, sales or some other area. Grooms take horses in and out of the barn and feed them. They also clean the animals and their stables. Grooms can give injured horses immediate first aid until the farm's **equine** veterinarian can treat the animal. In addition, the farm has employees who operate computers, keep financial records, and promote the farm's business.

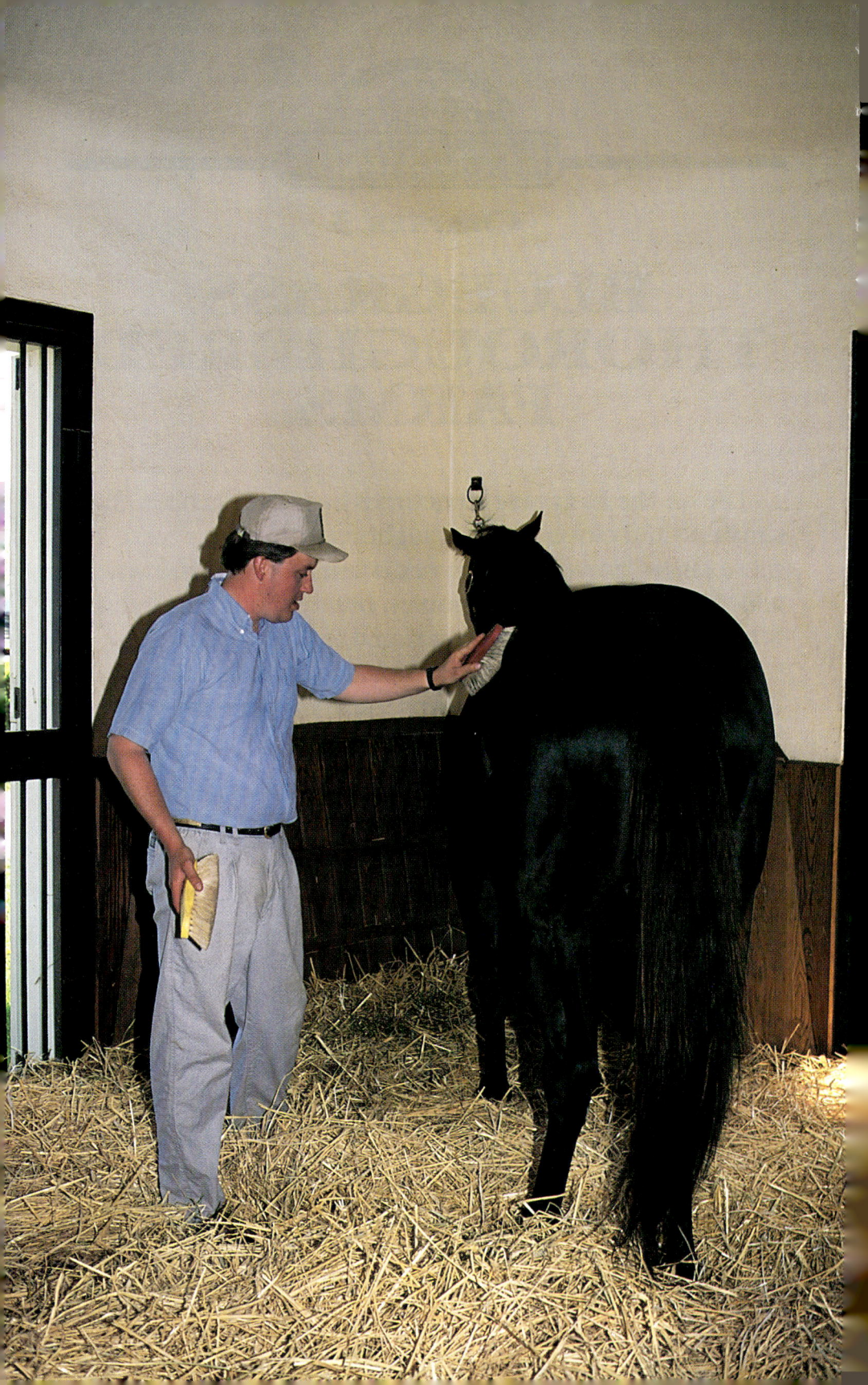

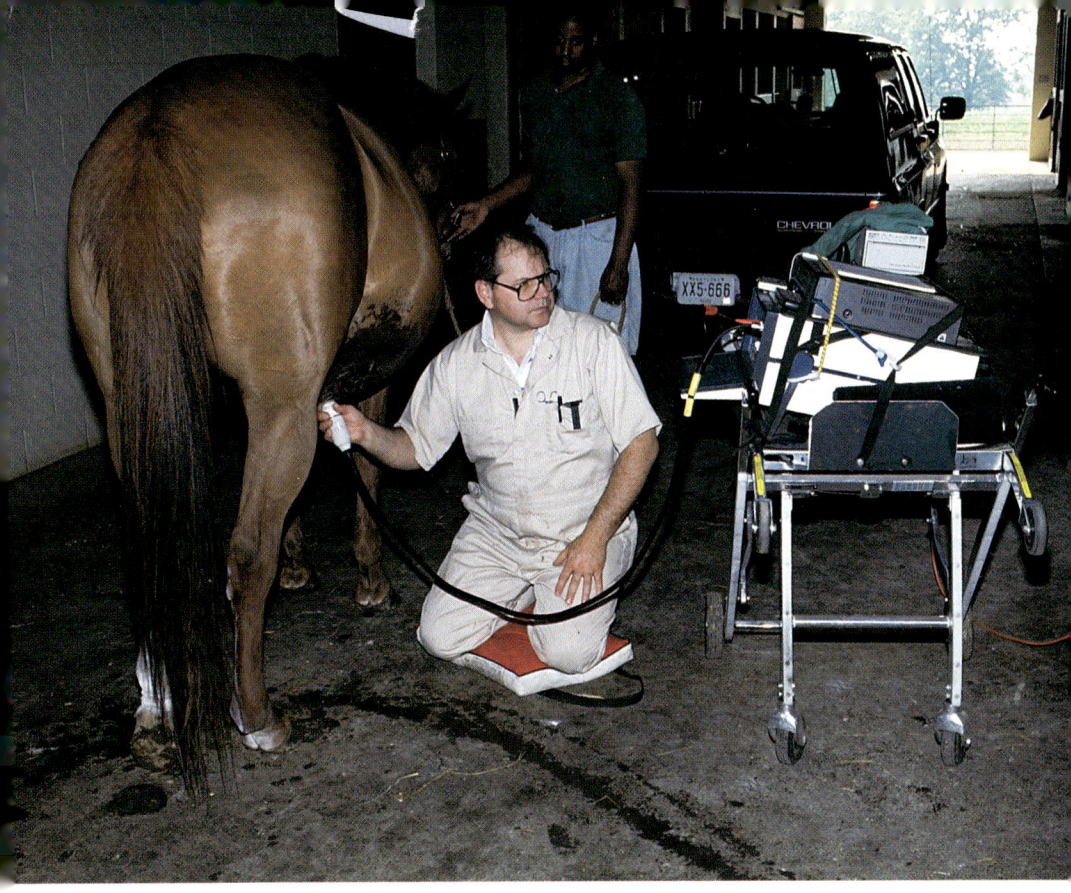

*An ultrasound device helps an equine veterinarian - a horse doctor - monitor a mare's pregnancy*

**Commercial** thoroughbred farms board and manage horses for many owners. A horse's owner, the farm's **client,** pays the farm for boarding its horse. A client may hire the farm for other purposes, too, such as the sale or purchase of a horse at public auction. Private farms raise horses for the farm owner's personal stable. Commercial farms may own horses, but their emphasis is on the boarding, buying and selling of other people's animals.

*Grooming champion thoroughbred stallions is a daily chore at Bluegrass thoroughbred farms*

*A champion stallion like Black Tie Affair - Horse of the Year in 1991 and now retired to the Vinery Farm - has a greater chance of siring top racehorses than a lesser stallion would.*

*Computers store a wealth of information about a thoroughbred's family history. That helps breeders match the best stallions with the best mares – and hope for the best.*

*Thoroughbreds are bought and sold at public auctions, like this one sponsored by the Keeneland Association*

Thoroughbred farms may raise mares only, or have mares and a few **stallions** – adult male horses. Stallions that have been racing champions are extremely valuable, sometimes worth millions of dollars. A thoroughbred owner knows that a former champion is more likely than an ordinary stallion to father a new champion. Eager to mate their best thoroughbred mares with champion stallions, the owners of mares sometimes pay more than $100,000 in **stud fees.** A stud fee is the amount of money that the owner, or owners, of a stallion charges for having that animal **sire,** or father, a **foal,** the baby horse. In the mid-1980s, stud fees sometimes topped $1 million!

*The great Seattle Slew, winner of thoroughbred racing's Triple Crown in 1977 and retired at Three Chimneys Farm, is a legend on hoofs*

Matching a great stallion and mare, even with the help of computer records, does not guarantee a future champion. Chance is the essence of horse racing and horse breeding. The chances of a stallion and a mare producing a champion are greatly increased when the parents, the sire and **dam,** or mother, are selected carefully by the breeders. The animals' physical qualities, ancestry and racing records are all considered in the matchmaking process.

A champion racing stallion may be retired from the track long before his racing days are spent. The greatest stallions are usually the earliest to be retired. A horse can begin racing as a two-year-old. He is usually finished by age five or six, but some race until they are nine and 10. The great Secretariat, for example, was retired after finishing his three-year-old season. By then, after just two years on the track, Secretariat had established himself as a legend. He was worth more to his owners as a sire than as a racer. An active racehorse always risks the chance of injury – or even death – on the track. After a stallion has retired to sunshine and clover, he may produce foals for more than 20 years and live to be about 30.

Racing and raising thoroughbreds is clearly a business – but it is also a labor of love, and it has a gentle side. The people who work with thoroughbreds often describe them with affection, as if they were talking about their children. Horses are "gentle," "kind," "sweet," "spirited," "smart." Horse cemeteries also testify to the genuine respect these animals earn from their owners.

*The equine cemetery at Calumet Farm honors the memories of the stable's remarkable run of champions*

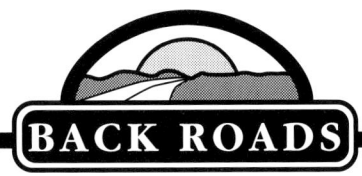

## Chapter 4
# BORN TO RUN

A thoroughbred foal is usually born between January and June. The foal can stand almost immediately, and within a few hours it bounds along at its mother's side. By the time it is a **yearling,** one year old, the young horse has reached about half of its adult size. A thoroughbred generally attains full adult size at the age of five. An adult thoroughbred weighs 1,000 to 1,300 pounds and stands 15 to 17 **hands** (60 to 68 inches) tall at the shoulder.

No one knows at first whether a young thoroughbred has championship potential. When they are about 18 months old, nearly all thoroughbreds are shipped to a racetrack or training center. There a trainer begins to condition a young horse to the saddle. Thoroughbreds are not broncos. They are handled by people almost from the moment they are born. "It's a matter of teaching them manners," says a Bluegrass groom. By the time a trainer begins saddle training, a young horse is already accustomed to being led and handled.

Thoroughbreds race in many different classes or levels, mostly determined by the skill and sex of the horse. A trainer can usually evaluate a horse's potential for racing when it is a two-year-old. Horses that mature late may not develop their talent until they are three or four.

*Trainers begin work with thoroughbreds at racetracks and training centers when the horses are about 18 months old*

Not every thoroughbred is fit for competitive racing. These horses are still in demand as hunters, jumpers, show horses and saddle mounts. A thoroughbred named Jet Run was so slow "he couldn't get out of his own way," a farm manager recalled, "but he became an Olympic jumping champion."

*Most thoroughbred foals are born between January and June, but, to simplify racing classes, all of them are officially considered one-year-olds - yearlings - on January 1 following their birthday.*

*A thoroughbred foal is the product of parents that have been carefully chosen by the breeder. The parents' speed, stamina, soundness and physical type are all factors in their selection.*

Like people, say Bluegrass folks, horses are different. Not all thoroughbreds that can race competitively do. Some thoroughbreds have the ability, but not the spirit – or what horse people call "heart." Not every horse has the desire to run past every other horse on a track. As Dan Rosenberg, general manager of the Three Chimneys Farm, says, "A horse has to want to win, to look another horse in the eye and say, 'You're not going to pass me.' "

Most horses in the major races are males. They generally have advantages over females in size, stamina and speed. Young male horses between the ages of two and five are known as **colts.** After age five they become "horses" in racing **jargon.** A male horse that has had its reproductive organs removed is a **gelding.** Horses are often gelded so that they will be easier to handle. A high-spirited stallion may be difficult to train and ride.

Female thoroughbreds are called yearlings as one-year-olds, and fillies between the ages of two and five. A **filly** becomes a mare when she reaches five.

*High-spirited stallions can sometimes be great runners, but difficult animals to focus, handle and train*

*An exercise rider at Three Chimneys Farm helps Chief's Crown, a retired champion, stay in shape*

## Chapter 5

# THOROUGHBREDS

Nature's gift to horses was speed. Long, strong legs, large lungs and a powerful heart helped keep the wild species of horses a nose or two ahead of big cats and other toothy characters with a taste for horse meat. Thousands of years ago, people captured wild horses for use as riding and work animals. Never quite satisfied with the wild types, human beings wanted to "improve" their horses. Wild horses were not all alike. Some were larger than others. Once in awhile, a horse would be exceptionally fast or long-legged. So the ancient peoples began to arrange mates for their horses. By mating two fast horses, for instance, they were likely to produce a foal that would grow up to be just as fast as its parents – or faster. People thus bred their horses selectively. The horses selected for breeding had the characteristics the breeders wanted to keep or exaggerate.

Selective breeding of horses has gone on for perhaps 5,000 years. Most modern-day **breeds,** or types, are somewhat removed from wild ancestors like the Przewalski's horse of Asia. The horses developed by human beings are not necessarily *better,* but they are certainly more *useful* for human purposes than, say, zebras or Przewalski's horses would be.

Selective breeding requires tradeoffs. To make a draft, or work, horse, the breeder selects for size and strength.

31

In turn, the breeder sacrifices speed. And each desirable feature that is bred into a horse's **conformation** - its shape, the way it's put together - may result in an undesirable characteristic appearing. Thoroughbreds, for example, have certain mechanical advantages in their conformation to enhance their running ability. The downside is that thoroughbred mares, because their conformation has affected the shape of their pelvic region, have a more difficult time bearing live foals than many other breeds.

*Belgian draft horses, like these at the Kentucky Horse Park, were selectively bred for size and strength*

Over 150 horse breeds are recognized today. The largest of them is a draft horse, the shire. Shires and some of the other draft breeds top 2,000 pounds. At the other extreme, selective breeding has produced the Falabella horse, so small that it could be mistaken for a German shepherd with a mane.

Until fairly recently, people were not concerned about keeping their horses purebred, or of blood from a single breed. At least they did not keep records to prove their horses' ancestry. That changed with the arrival of thoroughbreds, whose owners established a registry, a record of the animals' bloodlines.

All thoroughbreds' bloodlines can be traced to three Arabian stallions that were imported by breeders in England in the late 1600s and early 1700s. By crossing their saddle horses with the Arabians, the English developed the thoroughbred. Selective breeding for the next 150 years or so built up the thoroughbred's size, stamina and speed.

You cannot tell a thoroughbred by its color. It may be gray, black or various shades of brown – bay, chestnut or roan. Under their coats, however, thoroughbreds share such physical characteristics as large muscles in their upper legs and long, slim lower legs.

On a standard track, the thoroughbred is royalty – the fastest horse in the world.

*This mare and her foal are brown, or dark bay, one of several thoroughbred colors*

## CHAPTER 6
# OFF TO THE RACES

Thoroughbred races follow certain customs and standards. Nearly all thoroughbred races in the United States are held on a flat, oval track. The track, or course, may be grass, but most of them are dirt, which has a faster surface. The length of a race is usually from five-eighths of a mile to one and one-half miles. Tracks are measured in **furlongs.** Each furlong is one-eighth of a mile. The famous Kentucky Derby is a one and one-quarter mile (10-furlong) race.

Each horse is ridden by a jockey who weighs about 110 pounds. The jockey carries a whip and wears boots, a safety helmet, and a bright, silky jacket and cap. The jacket and cap, known as **silks,** have colors and a distinct design that identify the owner of the horse.

More people attend horse races than any other sport in America. Once known as the Sport of Kings, horse racing has fans from all reaches of society. Many of them wager, or bet, on which horses will finish first, second and third in each race. A race may have eight or 10 horses or more. The Kentucky Derby matches up to 20. Billions of dollars are wagered on horse races each year. The money wagered on a race becomes the **purse.** In some races, horse owners contribute to the purse.

*Thoroughbreds racing on Keeneland's turf, or grass, track in Lexington*

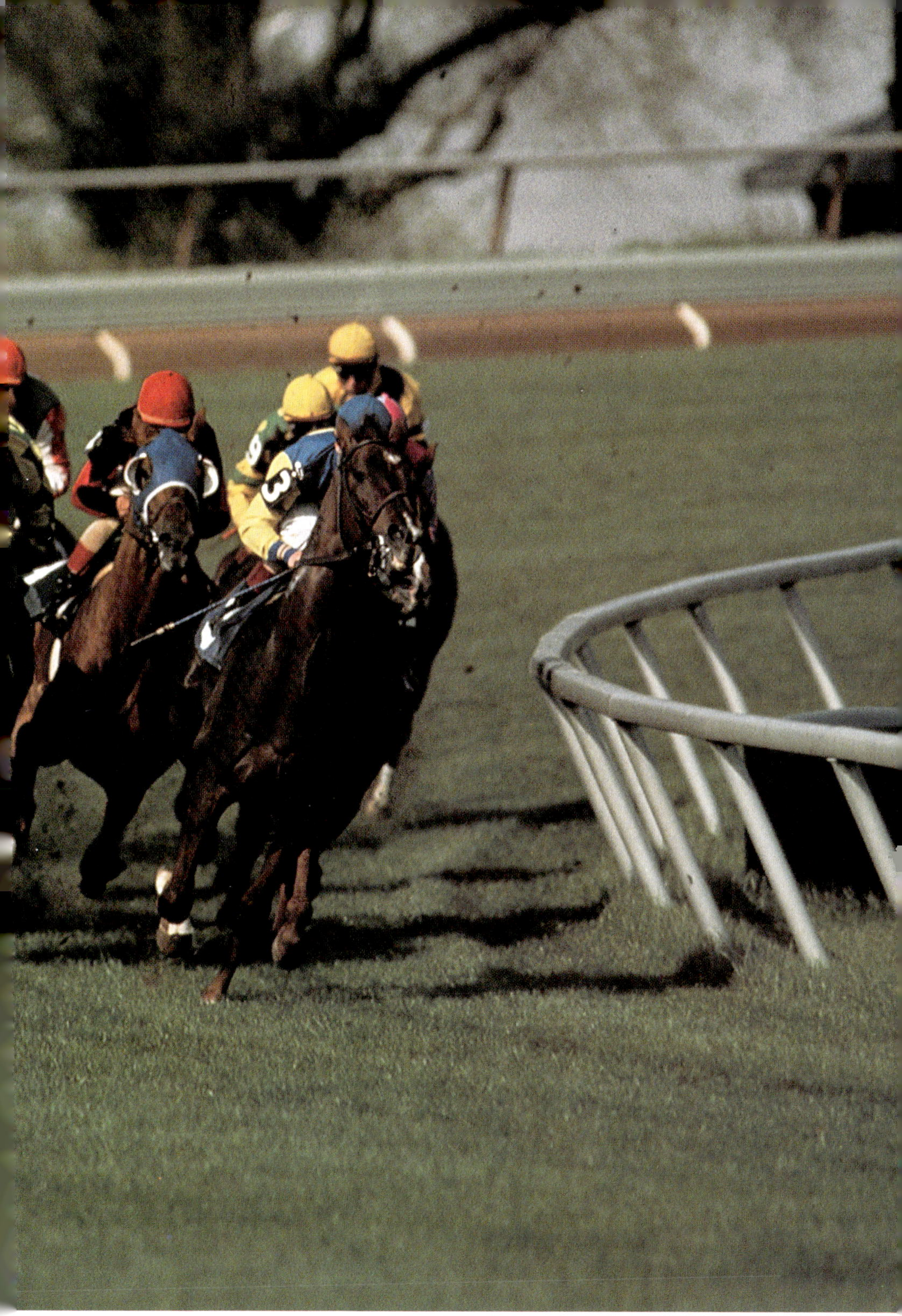

The purse is divided after a race. Horses that finish first through fourth win part of the purse. The track takes a percentage, and the state in which the race is run takes a cut. Most of the purse is divided among the people who wagered on the horses that finished first through third.

Racehorses travel in a circuit, moving from one racetrack to another with the season. Being born and raised in the Bluegrass region of Kentucky doesn't mean that a horse will ever race there, although that is a possibility. Two of the most famous tracks in America – Churchill Downs in Louisville and Keeneland in Lexington – are in Kentucky. Churchill Downs is the site of the annual Kentucky Derby. This race for outstanding three-year-olds began in 1875, and it has been held every year since. The Derby is the centerpiece of the three most celebrated thoroughbred races in the United States. The Preakness, started in 1873, and the Belmont Stakes, dating to 1867, round out the threesome. Together they are known as racing's Triple Crown. Occasionally a superb horse, such as Secretariat or Seattle Slew, captures all three races.

"The process of getting a horse to the races is beautiful, intriguing, filled with drama," said a Bluegrass racing man. "That's the appeal as much as anything else. To be able to compete with the chance to win is great, but you'd better be able to lose, because you'll lose far more often than you'll win."

## BACK ROADS

### Chapter 7

# THE KENTUCKY HORSE PARK

The state of Kentucky long ago hitched its image to the horse and the bluegrass. Kentucky is the Bluegrass State, and a horse appears on its automobile license plates. Another horse, a magnificent, winged horse – unusual even by Kentucky standards – hangs suspended from the ceiling of the Louisville airport terminal. A Frenchman, Francois Michaux, who visited the Bluegrass region in 1802, wrote, "If a traveler arrives, his horse is valued as soon as they see him." An English traveler to the region in 1819 observed that "Kentucky horses are the best in the United States."

In 1972 the state decided to give its reputation a boost. Kentucky bought part of a horse farm a short distance north of Lexington. When the state finished grooming the farm in 1978, Kentucky Horse Park emerged. Spacious and comfortable, Kentucky Horse Park celebrates the horse and the ongoing love affair people have with horses. For horse lovers, the park is highly entertaining and instructive. Part of the horse park's charm is its working farm atmosphere and opportunities for close encounters with horses. Horses with riders and draft horses pulling

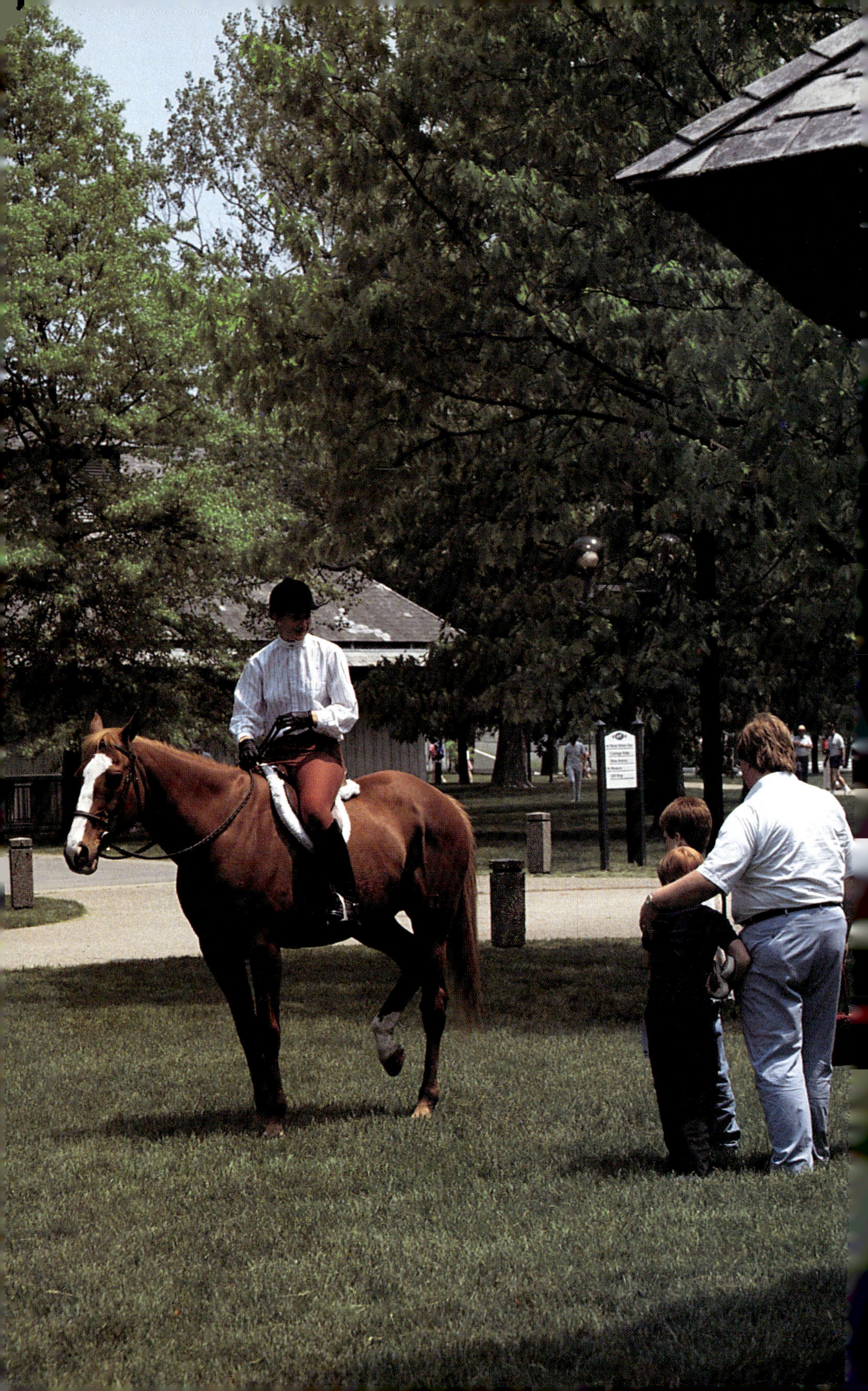

*A Lipizzan and its rider perform during the Parade of Breeds at Kentucky Horse Park*

wagons share the walkways with visitors. No one leaves the park without have been nose-stroking close to horses. The horses seem to enjoy the attention and their surroundings almost as much as their human admirers do.

The park has 32 miles of white-planked fences around its pastures and **paddocks.** Visitors can stroll leisurely along the fences, ride in a horse-drawn wagon, or opt to climb aboard a saddle horse and follow a shaded lane.

The clang of hammer on steel draws people to the **farrier** shop. Here the farrier, or blacksmith, hammers out shoes for horses and fits them to the animals. Next door is an arena where several featured horse breeds are shown individually in daily exhibitions called the Parade of Breeds. The park has about 40 breeds on display, including Belgians, percherons, thoroughbreds, Morgans, Lipizzans, appaloosas and quarter horses. Visitors can see the horses close-up in their stables, in the arena and elsewhere on the grounds.

*Close encounters with thoroughbreds and many other breeds are part of the fun at the Kentucky Horse Park*

**BACK ROADS**

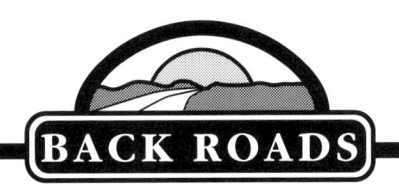

CHAPTER 8

# THE TRACK IN THE BLUEGRASS: KEENELAND

The Keeneland Association's racetrack is the Bluegrass Country's own. For many people Keeneland's tradition, ivy-covered brick walls and parklike grounds are reasons enough to attend the track's brief spring and fall racing meetings. Others love the pageantry and color of racing there – or they just enjoy seeing thoroughbreds with manes and tails streaming like banners in the wind. Hal Price Hadley, a founder of Keeneland, said in 1937, "We want a place where those who love horses can come and picnic with us and thrill to the sport of the Bluegrass. ... We don't care whether the people who come here bet or not. If they want to bet, there is a place for them to do it. But we want them to come out here to enjoy God's sunshine, the fresh air, and to watch horses race."

On an early morning in May, Keeneland quietly captures the soul of the Bluegrass Country. Like a dark serpent, the oval track lies in the gray light of dawn. The grandstand, the roofed structure from which spectators view a race, looms empty by the track. The first shafts of light sneak through a king's forest of Keeneland trees, and ribbon the dirt track and guardrail. It would be a magnificent stage in the dim light even without its cast, but the cast is here – thoroughbreds, trainers, jockeys, owners and grooms.

*In the first glow of an early morning in May, a thoroughbred and rider gallop briskly around the Keeneland track*

People of all racing stripes gather here, and the racing community discovers some of its champions-to-be. The activity of horses and riders, coming and going, is constant, but never chaotic. Patience is a virtue when one is dealing with thoroughbreds.

In ones and twos thoroughbreds from the Keeneland stables move like shadows onto the dirt track. Fidgety, lightning in a bottle, the horses stand, walk or canter at the jockey's wishes. Now and then a jockey sets the lightning free, and a thoroughbred thunders at nearly 30 miles per hour along the rail.

The morning spectacle at Keeneland is not reserved. It is open to anyone. Early-rising visitors mingle with horses and horse people. They press against the rail, sip coffee in the cool air, and watch champions being made in Bluegrass Country.

*White fences, grassy paddocks and white horses on a spring morning in the Bluegrass Country*

# Glossary

**breed** – a particular type of domestic animal with characteristics that separate it clearly from other animals of the same kind (*thoroughbred* horses as distinct from *Belgian* horses)

**canebrake** – a field of cane stalks

**client** – a person who hires another for professional services

**colt** – a male horse between the ages of two years and five years

**commercial** – relating to business and profit-making

**conformation** – the overall shape of an animal

**crossbreed** – an animal that is produced by parents of two distinct breeds, such as a foal with a *thoroughbred* mother and a *quarter horse* father

**dam** – a horse that bears a foal

**equine** – relating to horses

**farrier** – a blacksmith; one who shoes horses

**filly** – a female horse between the ages of two years and five years

**foal** – a baby horse prior to the age of one year

**furlong** – a unit of measurement equal to one-eighth of a mile

**gelding** – a male horse whose reproductive organs have been removed

**groom** – a stable worker

# GLOSSARY

**hand** – a unit of measurement for determining the height of horses; equal to four inches

**jargon** – a specialized vocabulary

**native** – a plant or animal that is natural to a place

**paddock** – an outdoor enclosure in which horses are kept

**purebred** – an animal bred from members of one recognized breed

**purse** – the money collected by the ractrack before a race, and then distributed after it is run

**savannah** – a natural, parklike expanse of grass and some trees

**silks** – the colorful, silky jacket and cap worn by a jockey

**sire** – a male horse that fathers a foal

**stallion** – an adult male horse

**stud fee** – the money charged by a horse breeder for a stallion to sire a foal

**yearling** – a thoroughbred colt or filly on the January 1 following its birth and until the next January 1, after which it is a two-year-old

# INDEX

agriculture  11
American Civil War  11
barns  9, 15
beef cattle  7
Belmont Stakes  38
blacksmith (see *farrier*)
bluegrass  8, 9, 10, 11, 39
Bold Ruler  5
breeders  33
breeds  31, 32, 33, 41
canebrakes  10
cattle  11
cattle farms  9
cemeteries (for horses)  22
Churchill Downs  38
Claiborne Farm  5
colts  28
conformation  32
draft horse  31, 33, 39
England  11, 33
farrier  41
farrier shop  41
fences  9, 41
fillies  28
foals  20, 22, 24, 31, 32
forest  10
furlongs  35
gelding  28
grasses  11
grooms  15, 24, 42
Hadley, Hal Price  42
Harrodsburg, KY  10
hemp  11
historic districts  10
horse farms  5, 9, 12, 15, 17, 20
Horse of the Year  5
horse races  28, 35, 38
horse racing  11, 22, 25, 35, 42
horses  8, 9, 11, 15, 28, 39, 41, 42, 44
  American saddlebred  5
  appaloosa  41

Arabian  5, 33
Belgian  41
Falabella  33
Lipizzan  41
Morgan  5, 41
percheron  41
Przewalski's  31
quarter horse  5, 41
shire  33
standardbred  5
thoroughbred  5, 9, 12, 15, 22, 24, 28, 32, 33, 41, 42, 44
hunters  25
Inner Bluegrass region  5, 7
jockeys  35, 42, 44
jumpers  25
Keeneland  38, 42, 44
Keeneland Association  42
Kentucky  5, 10, 11, 38, 39
Kentucky Derby  35, 38
Kentucky Horse Park  39, 41
legs  33
Lexington, KY  5, 7, 9, 12, 38, 39
limestone  5
Louisville, KY  38
mares  20, 22, 28, 32
Maryland  11
Michaux, Francois  39
muscles  33
National Register of
  Historic Places  10
owners  15, 42
paddocks  41
Parade of Breeds  41
pioneers  10, 11
*Poa pratensis* (see *bluegrass*)
Preakness  38
public auction  17
purse  35
race, racing (see *horse races, horse racing*)
racehorses  4, 22, 38

47

# INDEX

racetrack   24, 33, 35, 38, 42, 43
Rosenberg, Dan   28
savannahs   10, 11
Seattle Slew   38
Secretariat   5, 22, 38
selective breeding   31
sheep   7
shoes   41
silks   35
soil   10
stables   9, 15, 41
stallions   20, 22, 28
stud fee   20
thoroughbred farm (see *horse farms*)
Three Chimneys Farm   28
tobacco   4, 7, 9, 11
track (see *racetrack*)
trainers   24, 42
trees   8, 9, 10, 13, 42
Triple Crown   38
veterinarian   15
villages   9
Virginia   5, 10, 11
yearling   24, 28
zebras   31